THE 10™

Hottest Hollywood Cars

Glen Downey • Maria Malara

Series Editor
Jeffrey D. Wilhelm

Much thought, debate, and research went into choosing and ranking the 10 items in each book in this series. We realize that everyone has his or her own opinion of what is most significant, revolutionary, amazing, deadly, and so on. As you read, you may agree with our choices, or you may be surprised — and that's the way it should be!

Franklin Watts®

an imprint of

SCHOLASTIC

www.scholastic.com/librarypublishing

A Rubicon book published in association with Scholastic Inc.

Rubicon © 2008 Rubicon Publishing Inc.
www.rubiconpublishing.com

Associate Publishers: Kim Koh, Miriam Bardswich
Project Editor: Amy Land
Editor: Jessica Calleja
Creative Director: Jennifer Drew
Project Manager/Designer: Jeanette MacLean
Graphic Designers: Waseem Bashar, Brandon Köpke, Doug Bains

The publisher gratefully acknowledges the following for permission to reprint copyrighted material in this book.

Every reasonable effort has been made to trace the owners of copyrighted material and to make due acknowledgment. Any errors or omissions drawn to our attention will be gladly rectified in future editions.

"The Italian Job: Press Conference with Charlize Theron and Mark Wahlberg" (excerpt). Permission courtesy www.viewlondon.co.uk.

"Hybrid cars gain star power" (excerpt) by Peter Viles, October 23, 2002. Permission courtesy CNN.com.

"James Bond's car stolen from Boca airport" (excerpt) by Claire Booth, June 20, 1997, *Boca Raton News*. Reprinted with permission of the South Florida Media Group, publisher of the *Boca Raton News* and in which this material originally appeared.

"Reinventing the Batmobile" (excerpt) by Ron Magid for *Popular Mechanics*, July 2005 (www.popularmechanics.com). Reprinted with permission.

Cover: *2 Fast 2 Furious* movie still–Photo by Eli Reed/Universal Studio/ KPA-ZUMA/KEYSTONE Press

Library and Archives Canada Cataloguing in Publication

Downey, Glen R., 1969–
      The 10 hottest Hollywood cars / Glen Downey, Maria Malara.

Includes index.
ISBN 978-1-55448-526-0

      1. Readers (Elementary). 2. Readers—Automobiles. 3. Readers—Motion pictures. I. Malara, Maria II. Title. III. Title: Ten hottest Hollywood cars.

PE1117.D6936 2007a   428.6   C2007-906699-2

1 2 3 4 5 6 7 8 9 10   10   17 16 15 14 13 12 11 10 09 08

Printed in Singapore

Contents

BURN RUBBER

Some blockbuster movies and hit TV shows are known for their edgy humor. Others become popular because of their good-looking stars. Many get noticed because of their state-of-the-art special effects. Then there are the ones that are all about the cars.

So, when you think of the entertainment world's most famous cars, what comes to mind? Let's face it, a car that clocks the fastest time is amazing enough, but Hollywood's hottest ride needs something extra-special to stand out from the rest of the pack. What if it had a bunch of cool spy gadgets, or could survive the most daring stunts? How about exotic accessories, or even a superhero driver? There are so many things that can make a car famous, including a legend about being cursed!

Whether it's the latest fully loaded model or a cool retro ride, a hot car makes a statement like nothing else can. In this book, we present what we think are the 10 hottest Hollywood cars. In ranking them, we noted their amazing features, smart gadgets, and cool accessories. We also considered their unique designs; their effects on the popularity of the shows or films they starred in; their impact on popular culture; and how long these cars continue to be talked about — even after the TV series has ended or after the movie was first released.

SO, REV UP YOUR ENGINES AND COME ALONG FOR THE RIDE. AS YOU CRUISE ALONG, ASK YOURSELF:

WHICH HOLLYWOOD CAR IS THE HOTTEST OF THEM ALL?

The Magnum P.I. *TV* series was so popular that it aired in Germany, Italy, Russia, South Africa, United Kingdom, and several Spanish-speaking countries.

RRARI

DEBUT: The first episode of *Magnum P.I.* aired in 1980 and the series ran for eight years.

MAKE/MODEL: Over the years three versions of the flashy red Ferrari were used in the series: a 1979 308 GTS, a 1981 308 GTSi, and a 1984 308 GTS QV.

It must have been great to be Magnum P.I. He was head of security for a massive estate owned by a world-famous author. He lived right by the ocean on a tropical island where it's summer 365 days a year. To top it all off, he got to drive around Hawaii in a sporty red convertible. Does life get any better than that?

Yet, it does! Magnum's convertible was no ordinary sports car. It was the best of the best — a Ferrari 308 GTS. There's definitely more to this hot car than looks. It is also a masterpiece of design, engineering, and technology. For more than 60 years, Ferrari has been creating some of the world's finest, fastest, and most desired sports cars.

Sleek and speedy, this red Ferrari won fans of its own while adding to the show's popularity. To this day, the red convertible Ferrari is known as "the Magnum P.I. car." In fact, some Ferrari fans think that Magnum gave the brand so much free publicity that part of the Ferrari factory should be named after him!

MAGNUM'S FERRARI

A STAR IS BORN

The sleek 308 GTS was a mid-engined sports car with a top speed of more than 150 mph. While Magnum's car was always a red, semi-convertible two-seater, three slightly different versions of the 308 were used for the show. Many people watched *Magnum P.I.* just so they could fantasize about cruising around Hawaii in this sporty ride.

IN THE DRIVER'S SEAT

Tom Selleck played the role of Thomas Magnum, a private investigator in charge of the security at a famous author's estate. As part of the perks, Magnum got to drive the often-absent author's Ferrari. The Ferrari had to be modified because Tom Selleck was too tall. The seat had to be bolted as far away from the steering wheel as possible to make room for his long legs!

mid-engined: *engine is located behind the passenger compartment to prevent the car from sliding*

TRENDSETTER

Thanks to *Magnum P.I.*, the Ferrari 308 was one of the Italian company's most popular models. The 308 was designed to look like the ultimate sports car. It's no accident that when people think of a sports car, Ferraris often pop into their minds. Its exotic looks are often imitated by many other car companies.

Quick Fact

In 2006, Ferrari sold 5,700 cars worldwide. Over 1,700 of these were sold in North America, which made it the company's most important market.

? North America makes up about 10% of the world's population, but accounts for 30% of Ferrari sales. What does this tell you about North American spending habits?

10   9   8   7   6

The Big 6-0

Read this report to find out how Ferrari celebrated in style.

In 2007, Ferrari celebrated its 60th birthday. The Italian company decided to honor this milestone in a very special way.

The celebration began at the Italian embassy in Abu Dhabi, capital of the United Arab Emirates. Ferrari owners set out on a relay that involved over 10,000 cars driving across China, Japan, Australia, South Africa, South America, North America, and all of Europe. During this trip, a special baton was passed bearing 60 enamel symbols. Each symbol represented the 60 most important events in Ferrari's history. It was topped by a platinum and diamond prancing horse — very Ferrari indeed.

At the start of the relay, Piero Ferrari, son of company founder Enzo, also announced that the company would build and sell 60 very unique 612 Scagliettis. The cars were made in colors of the brand's most popular models of years past. What made each 612 especially rare was a small enameled symbol, each matching one of the 60 symbols on the relay baton.

But wannabes couldn't drive up to the local Ferrari dealership and plunk down a deposit for one of these amazing rides. Hopeful owners had to be invited by the company to buy one — what else would you expect from Ferrari?

? Purchase by invitation only. What does that tell you about Ferrari cars?

The Expert Says...

"If someone said to me that you can have three wishes, my first would have been to get into racing, my second to be in Formula One, my third to drive for Ferrari."

— Gilles Villeneuve, Formula One race-car driver (1950–1982)

Take Note

Kicking off our list at #10, the Ferrari brand was already popular when it was unveiled as Magnum's main ride. But the combination of this hot car with this hot show introduced this Italian brand to the masses and made these cars a status symbol for the rich and famous.
- How do you think Ferrari's winning track record as a race car helped to make it more popular?

5   4   3   2   1

Three electric-powered Minis were built for the 2003 version of The Italian Job. This was because gas-powered vehicles are not allowed in the Los Angeles subway system.

M THE ITALIAN JOB

DEBUT: Minis were already cool when *The Italian Job* came out in 1969. Their cool factor more than doubled after the film's 2003 remake.

MAKE/MODEL: The 1969 film featured the classic Minis. The 2003 film showcased the new generation models.

There is nothing like a big sports car with a monster engine that can go from zero to 60 in a matter of seconds. You know, the kind of car that turns heads every time it's seen cruising down the street.

Enter the Mini Cooper — a small car with a big impact! This practical car has been called everything from "quaint" to "goofy" to "the most influential car in history outside of Ford's Model T."

In 2001, BMW launched a new, redesigned Mini. Shortly after its release, the new Mini starred in a remake of *The Italian Job*. Even the most serious film critics had to admit that these lively little cars stole the show.

MINI COOPER

A STAR IS BORN

This small wonder was originally designed to fight oil and gas shortages in the 1950s. At first, sales were slow. But when a few celebrities were seen in Minis, the practical little car suddenly became cool. Minis were manufactured by the British Motor Corporation until 2000. They were the pride of the British car industry and the most popular line of cars in Great Britain.

IN THE DRIVER'S SEAT

The Mini is the unlikely hero of *The Italian Job*. The movie starts off with a group of thieves pulling off a massive gold heist. But one of the thieves betrays the group, taking the gold for himself. To get it back, the others come up with a plan involving Minis. In a mind-blowing chase, three Minis impressively screech and swerve through L.A. traffic, the subway system, and even along Hollywood's Walk of Fame!

TRENDSETTER

Whether it's in a movie or on the street, there's something about the Mini that makes people smile. This cute package also revolutionized the way small cars were made. Engineers realized that moving the wheels all the way to the corners and turning the engine sideways increased passenger space. It also helped the Mini easily take even the tightest corners. Minis — old and new — have shown us that a small, practical car can still be stylish, unique, and really fun to drive!

1964 Mini Cooper

? Before the new Mini was designed, the original was around for almost 40 years without many changes in its design. Why do you think this is?

Quick Fact

The Mini is not considered a luxury car, but it still makes a big statement. This is one of the reasons why many celebrities, such as Clint Eastwood, James Blunt, Jennifer Love Hewitt, and each member of the Beatles, have been proud Mini owners.

2005 Mini Cooper

10   **9**   **8**   **7**   **6**

THE ITALIAN JOB: PRESS CONFERENCE

with Charlize Theron & Mark Wahlberg

Matthew Turner talks to the stars of *The Italian Job* in this interview from viewlondon.co.uk.

MATTHEW TURNER: Charlize, if I may start with you, it's been reported that of all the members of the cast, you were the best when it came to getting behind the steering wheel and driving a fast car, much to the chagrin of the gentleman sitting beside you and other male members of the cast. True or false?

CHARLIZE: I think you'd better ask Mark ...

MARK: Charlize had eight stunt doubles ... [Laughter]. No, she was certainly the most gung ho of all the cast members to get behind the wheel and she had some of the more challenging stunts to do, especially the sequence in the garage where we're preparing to do the first heist that goes awry, but she's definitely the daredevil of the group. But I am challenging her to a race right now — some journalist suggested we have a race for the release of the DVD.

CHARLIZE: I heard that. But why have a race when you know you'd have to stop to throw up and I would win, no matter what?

MARK: I only get carsick when I'm in the passenger seat of a stick shift ... and it's 120°F and I just had a sub for lunch. That's when I got sick.

CHARLIZE: It's always an excuse, isn't it, Mark? ...

chagrin: *embarrassment*

Quick Fact

In the final chase scene of *The Italian Job*, three Mini Coopers have the task of hauling $35 million in gold bars. As you might have guessed, although Minis are great cars, they could never really carry this heavy load.

The Expert Says...

"The Mini ... is more square than it is long, and the sight of those three squat, wheeled cubes, trundling and rolling resolutely over uncertain terrain, made for one of the original movie's purest visual delights."

— Stephanie Zacharek, film critic

resolutely: *with determination*

Take Note

Some cars stand for power, while others stand for wealth and even speed. The Mini Cooper proves that good things come in small packages and should not be underestimated. That's why it ranks #9 on our list.

• Imagine that you were asked to direct a film involving a car chase with a Mini. How would you film the car chase?

5   4   3   2   1

Hollywood is looking greener than ever thanks to the Environmental Media Association. This nonprofit organization gets TV and film producers to include environmental messages and products (such as hybrids) in their movies.

ECO

HYBRIDS

DEBUT: The late 1990s

MAKE/MODEL: Almost all the major car companies are producing hybrids that are powered by a combination of gas and batteries.

Okay, we'll admit the Toyota Prius probably won't win any beauty contests (especially when compared to the hot cars you've read about so far). That's why it's good to remember that with cars — as in life — it is what's under the hood that counts.

Hybrids are powered by a smaller version of the fuel-burning engine that's found in a regular car. This small engine is helped out by a battery-powered electric motor that gets charged while the car is running. This means hybrids require less fuel to go the same distance as regular cars. In addition to saving money on gas, hybrids conserve Earth's fossil fuels. They also produce less air pollution, which is a leading cause of global warming.

As the need to protect the environment becomes even more urgent, it's no surprise that these green cars have become automotive superstars. Hybrids are becoming red-carpet regulars, shuttling around stars like Cameron Diaz, Leonardo DiCaprio, and Orlando Bloom.

green: *environmentally friendly*

GAS-ELECTRIC HYBRIDS

A STAR IS BORN

What did it take to get people excited about this not-so-speedy car? We'd like to think it was the green factor, but it was actually star power. The Toyota Prius was launched in 1997 as the first mass-market gas-electric hybrid. Like the Mini, early sales were slow — at least until eco-conscious actor Leonardo DiCaprio was seen driving one. Then the rest was history!

IN THE DRIVER'S SEAT

It seems that more and more image-conscious celebrities are arriving at events in their hybrids instead of gas-guzzling limousines. Hybrids are also showing up on TV and in movies such as *In Her Shoes*, *The Last Kiss*, and *Scary Movie 3*. In a scene from the film *Be Cool*, a Hollywood producer shows up at an event in a hybrid car. When someone asks him about its lack of speed, he says, "If you're important, people will wait."

? Why do you think Hollywood stars would want to be seen driving hybrids instead of cars that run on gas alone?

TRENDSETTER

Our planet's weather is getting more unpredictable because of global warming. Glaciers are melting, droughts occur regularly, and the number of severe storms is on the rise. A major cause of global warming is the carbon dioxide gas created when cars burn fuel. A hybrid car releases around 4,338 pounds of carbon dioxide yearly. A large SUV releases around 14,815 pounds per year! Hybrids are a great start, but for the sake of our planet, we need to start coming up with cars that are even greener.

Quick Fact

Hybrid drivers get all sorts of perks! Some states offer tax rebates to hybrid owners, while some insurance companies give them discounts. In some cities, hybrid cars can park for free.

---

rebates: *sums of money returned to a customer*

? Do you think it's fair to regular car owners that only hybrid owners get such perks? Why or why not?

The Expert Says...

"Choosing a hybrid is something everyone can do today to help reduce our negative impact on the environment."

— Orlando Bloom, actor

8

Hybrid Cars gain ★ STAR POWER

An article from CNN.com
October 23, 2002
By Peter Viles

Cameron Diaz getting into her hybrid car

LOS ANGELES, California — California has the ultimate car culture — it is often said that there, you are what you drive.

California is also a capital of air pollution, and of efforts to cut down auto emissions. Put those three factors together and you have an unusual trend: a status symbol in reverse — a cool car that is not exactly a high-performance vehicle.

Car salesman Chris Cutright has sold so-called "hybrid" cars to many Hollywood stars. "I sold Cameron Diaz her car; Leonardo DiCaprio has bought three Prius from us; we're talking to Alec Baldwin right now, he's certainly interested in the car," Cutright said. …

Baldwin said: "The Prius is a great public relations veil, it's a shroud I can wear that will hide me. No one would ever dream I would be the guy behind the wheel of that car, that's great."

But in Los Angeles, you are what you drive … so what are you if you drive this quiet little car?

For Baldwin, "you're a genius with foresight, you are a far-seeing genius."

"Certainly somebody who's environmentally conscious," Cutright said.

shroud: *cover; disguise*
foresight: *ability to see ahead*

? If environmentally friendly vehicles are available, why do you think most car owners are still buying regular cars instead of hybrids?

Take Note

Hybrids take the #8 spot on our list. They may not look the coolest, but what's hotter than helping out the environment? It's not easy being green, though. Some of the drawbacks include lack of speed and expensive repairs.
• Compare the pros and cons of owning a hybrid car versus a regular gas-powered one. Which one would you choose and why?

5   4   3   2   1

7 FORD MUSTANG

As the star of one of the most legendary Hollywood car chases, this Mustang screamed through the streets of San Francisco at more than 105 mph.

FROM BULLITT

DEBUT: The 1968 movie *Bullitt*, starring Steve McQueen

MAKE/MODEL: A green Ford Mustang GT 390 fastback that had numerous modifications done to its shocks, suspension, and engine

Hybrids are nice, but let's shift gears and go back to the swinging '60s, back when it was okay to drive gas-guzzling hot rods with big powerful engines. These American muscle cars — especially the Ford Mustang — were the kings of the road. And a big part of their popularity came from an awesome car chase in the 1968 film *Bullitt*.

This intense chase through the streets of San Francisco lasted for under 10 minutes, but will be remembered forever. Gutsy police officer Frank Bullitt chases and gets chased by the bad guys who are driving another American classic — a 1968 Dodge Charger. Movie viewers had never seen anything so realistic. There's no background music and no dialogue. The focus is on heart-stopping action in the form of screaming engines, flying hubcaps, and squealing tires as the two cars burn rubber through the streets of San Francisco.

This scene changed the way filmmakers created action films. It also turned the fairly low-priced, but powerful, Ford Mustang GT 390 into one of the hottest cars the world has ever seen.

 Why do you think the director chose not to include music or dialogue in the famous chase scene? Think of similar scenes. Were they effective?

FORD MUSTANG

A STAR IS BORN

The first Mustang rolled off the assembly line in Dearborn, Michigan, on March 9, 1964. Four years later, the producers of *Bullitt* bought two Ford Mustang GT 390s. The suspension of each car was then modified to withstand all of the film's jumping stunts.

IN THE DRIVER'S SEAT

The 1968 Ford Mustang GT 390 was the perfect match for Frank Bullitt. This tough San Francisco cop was played by the equally tough actor Steve McQueen. Also known as "The King of Cool," McQueen was a real-life daredevil who raced cars and motorbikes. He often did his own stunt driving — but not in *Bullitt*. During shooting, McQueen lost control of the Mustang and the producers decided it would be safer to hire a stuntman.

suspension: *set of springs and shock absorbers that connect the car's wheels to its frame*

? How much of a role did Steve McQueen play in raising this car's cool image? When can a celebrity's influence be a bad thing?

TRENDSETTER

The incredible thing about *Bullitt* is that there were no special visual effects. When you see those cars crashing around corners at 105 mph, it is 100 percent real. Up to that point, films had never been made that way. *Bullitt* also turned the 1968 Mustang into an icon. As Steve McQueen said, "An audience digs sitting there watching somebody do something that I'm sure almost all of them would like to do."

Steve McQueen as Frank Bullitt — McQueen's real-life thrill-seeking made his many action-film roles even more intense.

Quick Fact

The roar of *Bullitt's* Mustang is actually from a NASCAR race car. It was added to the film's soundtrack because McQueen felt the standard Mustang sound was not powerful enough for the big screen.

The Expert Says...

" It was WILD reckless driving, but it was planned and coordinated. ... That's one of the key things people forget: the greatest stunt in the world is worthless if there isn't a reason or story to it and *Bullitt* had a story point all the way through and a reason. "

— Loren James, stunt worker

THE SEARCH FOR THE ORIGINAL BULLITT MUSTANG

This article explains the search for one of the most amazing pieces of movie memorabilia.

Two 1968 Mustangs were used for the filming of *Bullitt*. Once the Mustangs were chosen, they were modified for the high-speed chase scenes. They were outfitted with stronger springs and special shock absorbers, and had braces built into the inner fenders. Some minor tuning was also done to the engines.

After filming wrapped up, the main car was in bad shape. Two weeks of stunt driving had taken its toll on the Mustang, so it was sent to the crusher. The less-damaged backup was sold to an employee of the studio.

In the early 1970s, the car was advertised in a classified ad in the *Los Angeles Times*. A buyer was found and the car made its way to the east coast. The Mustang went up for sale again in 1974. Some say that Steve McQueen even called to buy the car himself. He was told it had been sold, but was given the name and number of the buyer.

McQueen tried to convince the new owner to sell it, but failed. The owner did promise to contact him if he ever changed his mind. But McQueen died in 1980 with no contact. The current owner has continuously refused offers of purchase or publicity.

The car stayed in New Jersey until the 1990s, until it was moved to a farm in the Ohio River Valley. Parked in a hay barn, the Mustang is not roadworthy and still wears New Jersey license plates. A film company's offer to the owner for its use in a movie was turned down.

Take Note

The Ford Mustang GT 390 fastback earns the #7 spot on our list. The film *Bullitt* changed our perception of cars and was also responsible for turning the Mustang into an American muscle-car legend.
- Think of a time when you saw something in a movie or on TV that really stood out. Explain what caught your attention.

5   4   3   2   1

Imagine spending $20,000 on your car's paint job! This happens all the time in the world of tricked out sports cars. It's a world where car lovers are eager to spend big money on transforming ordinary cars into jaw-dropping street racers. You know what we're talking about. The cars with the booming stereos, flashy paint, glowing neon — oh — and don't forget the supercharged 500-horsepower engines.

The popularity of these cars exploded in 2001, just after the release of the film called *The Fast and the Furious*. It was a modestly budgeted movie about the then-unknown sport compact racing scene. It was full of hot cars in some incredible chases, races, and crashes. When it became a blockbuster, Hollywood was surprised. Where did these strange-looking vehicles come from? How did they go so fast? And why on Earth would someone spend $100,000 fixing up a car that was worth less than $10,000?

The Fast and the Furious was an unbelievable and unexpected success that went on to spawn two sequels. The real world was introduced to the world of modified sport compacts and there was no going back. This subculture had suddenly become a part of pop culture and everyone wanted to create his or her own one-of-a-kind dream machine.

compact: *small and economical car*
subculture: *small social group within a population*

THE FURIOUS CARS

DEBUT: Hollywood's fascination with cars came back with a vengeance when *The Fast and the Furious* hit screens in 2001.

MAKE/MODEL: Just about every kind of modified street racer makes its appearance across three action-packed films.

Actors (from left) Amaury Nolasco, Paul Walker, and Michael Ealy in 2 Fast 2 Furious (2003). The other films in this franchise are The Fast and the Furious (2001) and, most recently, The Fast and the Furious: Tokyo Drift (2006).

THE FAST AND THE FURIOUS CARS

A STAR IS BORN

In *The Fast and the Furious*, Vin Diesel's character drives some good old American muscle — a 1970 Dodge Charger. Paul Walker's character drives a 1995 Mitsubishi Eclipse GT, which also has a major role in *2 Fast 2 Furious*. By the time *The Fast and the Furious: Tokyo Drift* rolled around, the cars were the true stars. More than 200 of them were custom-built for the film and were maintained by a staff of 40 full-time mechanics!

IN THE DRIVER'S SEAT

While the main characters are played by some of Hollywood's hottest stars, stunt drivers are the real heroes of these films. Who else could stay in control while driving 140 mph just inches away from other cars, walls, and even the edge of a cliff? Rhys Millen was the main stunt driver for *The Fast and the Furious: Tokyo Drift*. He is a world-renowned expert in drifting (a technique that involves sliding the car sideways through tight turns) and is a top rally driver.

rally: *type of car race that takes place on public roads*

TRENDSETTER

People hadn't been this excited about hot rods since the muscle-car craze that began shortly after World War II. *The Fast and the Furious* franchise had an influence on everything — from fashion to video games to music. Carmakers suddenly realized that these films were a great marketing tool and tried desperately to get their brands showcased in the sequels. The multibillion-dollar market for fancy accessories and engine parts also experienced record growth.

? How do you feel about brand names being featured in films? Has this ever influenced you to purchase a product?

Quick Fact

The first script was criticized by serious car enthusiasts because of technical errors with the presentation of certain cars and their parts. But this didn't seem to hurt the franchise at the box office. Worldwide, the three films have earned more than $6 billion!

enthusiasts: *strong supporters*

9 8 7 6

TOO FAST, TOO FURIOUS

There's nothing like the thrill of watching a movie featuring two or more hot cars racing through the streets. But this should only take place in movies and video games. Real-life street racing isn't cool. It's deadly and illegal. Throughout the years, several films have been blamed for glorifying street racing and unfortunately *The Fast and the Furious* is one of them.

Check out these powerful facts about death in the fast lane ...

In 2001, the U.S. National Highway Traffic Safety Administration reported the number of fatal crashes as a result of street racing increased 87 percent.

In the United States, for every 1,000 street racers, there are 49 innocent bystanders who are injured or killed.

Automobile accidents are the leading cause of death for people aged 16 to 20.

Beat the Heat is a North American program that brings teens and police officers together to modify cars and even race against one another — on racetracks of course!

When a street race goes wrong, the results can be deadly.

Several factors contribute to the high number of auto accidents among teenagers. What are they? What can be done to get teens to drive safely?

The Expert Says...

"There's some undeniable appeal to watching a well-oiled, built-for-speed machine operating with its pedal to the metal."

— Mark Caro, film critic,
Chicago Tribune

Take Note

It's hard to ignore three amazing films full of so many hot cars. That's why *The Fast and the Furious* cars race in at #6. These high-performance vehicles, coupled with the films' success in reintroducing us to what tuned-up cars can do, put this entry ahead of the previous cars on our list.
• Do you think that having so many cars in a movie makes more of an impression than having only one car? Give at least three reasons to support your answer.

5   4   3   2   1

Does this car give you bad vibes? One of James Dean's friends said it looked sinister and warned him against driving it. How was Dean to know his friend would be right?

PORSCHE

DEBUT: 1953

MAKE/MODEL: The Porsche 550 Spyder was designed strictly for auto racing.

Ah, the life of a Hollywood actor on the brink of stardom. The year was 1955 and 24-year-old James Dean had gone from being a struggling actor to a star in three films. The films were just about to be released and there was a feeling that he was going to make it big.

When he wasn't acting, one of Dean's hobbies was racing cars. In fact, he had just used some of his movie money to treat himself to a new Porsche 550 Spyder. On September 30, 1955, Dean and his mechanic were on their way to a race in Salinas, California. They usually towed the car on a trailer. This time, though, Dean decided to practice driving the new car. At around 3:30 that afternoon, Dean was ticketed for going about 10 mph over the speed limit.

A couple of hours later, another car turned into the path of the speeding Spyder. Dean died almost instantly in the crash. His horrific death at a young age, combined with his incredible magnetism and talent, turned Dean into a Hollywood legend. The Porsche 550 Spyder became forever associated with his name.

JAMES DEAN'S PORSCHE

After his death, James Dean was nominated for Academy Awards for his roles in East of Eden (1955) and Giant (1956).

A STAR IS BORN

The 550 Spyder was the first Porsche designed specifically for auto racing. It was a two-seater with an open top and 110-horsepower engine. That might not seem like a lot after reading about the cars at #6, but the Spyder didn't weigh very much. This meant it could reach high speeds quickly because the engine didn't have to overcome a lot of inertia. The Spyder was so powerful that it often beat bigger rides on the racing circuit.

IN THE DRIVER'S SEAT

Even though James Dean has been dead for more than 50 years, people are still fascinated by him. He had a brief film career, but it made a huge impact on Hollywood. Actors are still trying to copy his trademark squint and angry mumbling. His role in *Rebel Without a Cause* caught the attention of post-war America's misunderstood teens. As biographer Joe Hyams wrote, "In some movie magic way, he managed to dramatize brilliantly the questions every young person in every generation must resolve."

inertia: *tendency to remain at rest unless acted on by an outside force*

TRENDSETTER

The 550 Spyder will always be remembered as the car that took James Dean to his tragic death. There's more to its history than tragedy, though. This legendary, mid-engined sports car brought Porsche many racetrack victories. Porsche did not forget the Spyder's importance. Its design was the inspiration for the Boxster, released in 1996. A few years later, the company released a special edition Boxster in recognition of the Spyder's 50th anniversary.

? Do you think Porsches would be as popular if James Dean had never driven one? Why or why not?

Quick Fact

Police officers said that the glare from the setting sun blinded the driver who hit Dean's Spyder. The actor's last words are said to have been, "That guy's gotta stop. He'll see us."

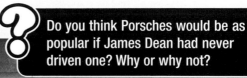

THE CURSE OF JAMES DEAN'S CAR

This article tells the spooky tale ...

James Dean's accident came as quite a shock to the world. But since his death, his Porsche 550 Spyder has been involved in many other accidents that hint this car may have been destined for tragedy.

George Barris, who did much of the custom work on the car, ended up buying the wreck. When it was brought to the garage, the car ended up sliding off the track and breaking both legs of the mechanic who was unloading it.

Barris ended up selling a few parts of the car to two racers. While racing against each other, one man crashed and died. The other was seriously injured when his vehicle rolled over.

Later on, two thieves were injured while trying to steal parts from the car. One tried to take the steering wheel, but a piece of jagged metal cut a deep gash into his arm. Another man was injured while trying to steal the front seat.

Barris thought it would be a good idea to loan the wrecked car to a highway safety exhibit. The garage storing the Spyder went up in flames, destroying everything except the car. On another occasion, the car fell from where it was being displayed and broke a student's hip. This unlucky auto also caused trouble while being moved. The truck that was transporting it lost control, causing the driver to fall out, only to have the Porsche fall on top of him.

The Porsche was last used in an exhibit in 1959. In 1960, when it was being returned to Barris, it mysteriously vanished. The car hasn't been seen since.

Dean's 550 Spyder was completely mangled beyond repair.

The Expert Says...

"[A Porsche] is like driving a go-cart. You sneeze and you're in the next lane."

— Richard Boutin, Porsche owner

Take Note

James Dean's Porsche 550 Spyder takes the #5 spot on our list. It had an impact on the development of Porsche as a company and also on James Dean's status as a Hollywood icon.
• Think of other celebrities who have died at a young age. Why do you think society tends to idolize famous people who die before their time?

5   4   3   2   1

Over 70 Herbie cars were produced for the filming of all five movies. Fewer than one-third exist today. Most of them were destroyed or badly damaged during stunt scenes.

LOVE BUG

DEBUT: Herbie has appeared in five films since 1969.

MAKE/MODEL: Herbie is "played" by a white 1963 Volkswagen Beetle.

This car has personality. This car has feelings. This car can even drive itself! But don't dismiss the Herbie movies as silly kid stuff just yet. Did we mention that this cute little Volkswagen took on a 2005 NASCAR racer — and won?

Welcome to the magical world of Disney. Before the studio released the 2005 movie *Herbie: Fully Loaded*, Herbie made his big-screen debut in *The Love Bug* way back in 1969. In the 1960s, the VW Beetle was still pretty new in the United States. This was shortly after the glory days of muscle cars like the Mustang. You can imagine that quite a few people thought this little European car was pretty strange looking. But then *The Love Bug* hit the theaters and audiences fell in love with the car that had a mind of its own. In 1969, *The Love Bug* became the most popular film in the United States. The craze had begun. Suddenly, it seemed like everyone was driving a Volkswagen Beetle. By 1973, more than 16 million Beetles had been produced. This broke the record set by Ford's Model T!

HERBIE THE LOVE BUG

A STAR IS BORN

All Herbies have been based on a 1963 Volkswagen Beetle, model 117. It took a whole team of special effects and stunt people to bring Herbie to life. For *Herbie: Fully Loaded*, puppeteer Bob Short studied old Herbie movies to get an idea of Herbie's "facial" expressions. He then chose different eyebrow, bumper, and body positions to convey each of Herbie's emotions.

IN THE DRIVER'S SEAT

Herbie has had different drivers in several movies. In *Herbie: Fully Loaded*, the car is driven by Maggie, played by Lindsay Lohan. Maggie saves Herbie from the scrapyard and the two quickly form a connection. In some breathtaking race sequences, Herbie helps Maggie show the male-dominated NASCAR world what she's made of.

puppeteer: *person who operates puppets*

TRENDSETTER

The Beetle was designed mainly by Dr. Ferdinand Porsche. It was Porsche's dream to make a car that everyone could afford. When it was first released in Germany in the 1930s, it was a bargain at $400. At that time, most cars cost more than $1,000. When a newspaper compared the car to a beetle, the name stuck. In the late 1960s, *The Love Bug* movie pushed Beetlemania to its peak. Several decades later, the Volkswagen Beetle is still one of the most recognizable cars in history.

Quick Fact

More than 21.5 million original Beetles were produced from 1930 until 2003. When the new Beetle was released in 1998, it paved the way for other retro-inspired cars like the Mini and PT Cruiser.

? The Beetle stopped being produced in North America in the 1970s. It was reintroduced in the 1990s and regained popularity. Why do you think the Beetle enjoyed so much success with its reintroduction in the 1990s?

OEF·857

The Expert Says...

" I really was [a Herbie fan] growing up. Especially the original Love Bug. I remember really wanting my parents' car to be alive. ... I remember that kind of simplicity of really wanting to be friends with your car. "

— Angela Robinson, director of *Herbie: Fully Loaded*

THE EVOLUTION OF HERBIE

A total of five Herbie movies have been made since 1969. Check out this timeline to see how this punchy little car has changed over the years.

1969 – HERBIE: THE LOVE BUG

The stripes used in this first Herbie movie didn't extend over the valances and were a different shade of blue. They also used wide racing tires in racing scenes. One of the cars used in filming actually had a Porsche 356 engine.

1974 – HERBIE RIDES AGAIN

The racing stripe was switched to navy blue. Volkswagen logos were also seen on the car. Volkswagen thought Herbie was such a good marketing tool that they supported the movie and sold Herbie accessories in their showrooms.

1977 – HERBIE GOES TO MONTE CARLO

Herbie switched back to wide tires for racing. The front seats were also higher. This was to help hide the stunt driver in the back seat. A stunt car was used in the scene where Herbie performed a wheelie. It was made out of fiberglass and was actually shorter than a real Volkswagen Beetle!

1980 – HERBIE GOES BANANAS

A later model with more oval mirrors was used. Herbie also set a Guinness World Record for being the first car to drive over the Panama Canal.

2005 – HERBIE: FULLY LOADED

The seats were white, instead of gray. The front seats had also gone back to their regular height. Herbie could smile, frown, and blink because of movable accessories such as the bumper!

---

valances: *panels that continue below a car's front bumper*
wheelie: *balance on the two back wheels*

Herbie seen here in Herbie Rides Again

Herbie in Herbie: Fully Loaded

Take Note

Even though Herbie was not the biggest, fastest, or most expensive car on our list, he did have something unique — personality! Herbie takes the #4 spot because he wasn't just a powerful hunk of metal. His character had thoughts and feelings just like a person and he formed a special bond with all of his owners.
• How do you think Herbie's personality sets him apart from other cars on this list? Explain.

5   4   3   2   1

③ KITT

The show's producer Glen A. Larson borrowed the idea of KITT's hood-mounted scanner from one of his earlier projects, the science fiction show called Battlestar Galactica.

DEBUT: Knight 2000 and its onboard computer, KITT, raced onto television screens on September 26, 1982, in the popular show, *Knight Rider*.

MAKE/MODEL: Black T-top 1982 Pontiac Trans Am with numerous high-tech features.

It all started when a dying millionaire named Wilton Knight rescued a young undercover police officer named Michael Long, who had been shot in the face. After plastic surgery, Long had a new face, a new name, and a new mission. With his new identity as Michael Knight, he would fight for justice with an incredible super-car, the Knight Industries Two Thousand, better known as KITT.

Michael and KITT were a perfect match. The car was a sleek, black, customized Pontiac Trans Am that could cruise at 300 mph, leap up to 50 feet in the air, and was loaded with ultra-advanced features. Best of all, it could talk and had a personality all its own. KITT was also totally protective of Michael. He would call the car whenever he was in trouble and it would come crashing through walls to get him.

Michael Knight may have been the show's human star, but KITT was definitely the main attraction.

KITT

A STAR IS BORN

KITT was so much more than just a sleek, black Pontiac Trans Am. It was a crime-fighting machine that was fitted with a number of amazing features. Not only did the car have an armor coating that allowed it to withstand weapon fire, it could travel over 300 mph and even capture criminals all by itself. If KITT had to get anywhere fast, it switched on its impressive turbo boost. Like Herbie, KITT had human qualities — a personality and a mind of his own.

? Imagine that you could talk to your car. What would be the advantages of this? What would you use this technology for?

Actor David Hasselhoff did poorly at his first audition for the part of Michael Knight. He asked for another try and before the second audition he repeatedly yelled at himself in the mirror, "I am the Knight Rider, I am the Knight Rider!" He nailed the second audition and was hired.

Quick Fact

Michael Knight had an evil twin and nemesis called Garthe Knight. Even KITT had an evil double. Its name was KARR, which stood for Knight Automated Roving Robot.

IN THE DRIVER'S SEAT

KITT's driver was Michael Knight, played by actor David Hasselhoff. Knight was selected to be KITT's driver because of his self-defense training, intelligence, law enforcement experience, and his ability to work alone. Knight had a close bond with KITT and treated the car like his partner.

TRENDSETTER

The show's success meant that Pontiac found itself swamped with customer requests for black Firebird Trans Ams with T-tops, tan interiors, and red lights on the front bumper, just like KITT. Car manufacturers even began offering vehicles with digital light instruments and security systems using electronic voices. Even though *Knight Rider* aired its last episode in 1986, KITT has since appeared on many television shows, cartoons, songs, and even video games.

? In what other ways do you think KITT influenced cars of today?

The Expert Says...

" The closest most of us will get to a talking car is using a navigation system. "

— Amanda Wegrzyn, Cars.com

10   **9**   **8**   **7**   **6**

HUMAN TOUCH

What made the fictional KITT car so special was that it was built to be more like a person than a machine. This list explains the different senses that made the car seem human.

☑ **Think**

KITT was able to think, learn, communicate, and interact with humans because of an advanced microprocessor. The Knight 2000 microprocessor worked like KITT's "brain" and made the car self-aware.

☑ **See**

KITT's red front scanner was built from a fiber-optic collection of electronic eyes. The scanner could see in many wavelengths including X-ray and infrared.

☑ **Talk**

A voice synthesizer is what made KITT able to speak. KITT mainly spoke English, but could also speak in Spanish and French or with different accents.

☑ **Smell**

KITT could "smell" through atmospheric sensors that were mounted in its front bumper.

☑ **Touch**

Tiny audio and visual sensors were embedded into the grooves of KITT's body. They used visual tracking to sense anything that was around the car.

☑ **Hear**

A system of audio sensors were placed throughout the inside and outside of the car that allowed it to hear.

Quick Fact

In many of KITT's jump scenes, the screen usually cut to another angle (like Michael driving) before landing. This is because more often than not, the front end of the stunt car was destroyed upon landing.

Take Note

Crime-fighting KITT roars onto our list at #3. With all of its high-tech gadgets, KITT was way ahead of its time. The car became so popular that some people believe it overshadowed the show's star, David Hasselhoff.
• Do you really think it's possible for a car to steal the show? Why or why not?

5   4   **3**   2   1

Actor Daniel Craig (as James Bond) poses with the Aston Martin DBS he drove in the 2006 film Casino Royale.

ASTON MARTIN

DEBUT: James Bond first drove an Aston Martin in the 1964 film *Goldfinger*.

MAKE/MODEL: Bond has driven many different Aston Martin models throughout the years, but none created quite a stir as the DB5.

It was nearly 40 years ago that James Bond, then played by Sean Connery, was introduced to his silver Aston Martin DB5 in the 1964 film *Goldfinger*. It would prove to be a match made in Hollywood heaven.

The car got people talking, not only because of its timeless beauty, but also because of the tempting gadgets it was fitted with. It was one of the silver screen's first tricked out cars with a collection of fantastic gadgets — ejector seats, smokescreens, machine guns, and secret compartments. In the latest movie, *Casino Royale*, the car had a secret first-aid kit that could analyze Bond's blood to find out what poison was in his system.

Throughout the years, Bond has tested out different makes and models, but he always somehow finds his way back into the original Aston Martin. This powerful and classy car has proven to have its own unique character to match that of James Bond.

JAMES BOND'S ASTON MARTIN

A STAR IS BORN

The Aston Martin DB5 was released in 1963. Introduced in *Goldfinger*, the Aston Martin is the most famous and most recognized James Bond car. Like Bond, the Aston Martin's design is the perfect balance of elegance and strength. The car used in the film was the original DB5 prototype, with another car used for stunts. Other Bond films featuring Aston Martins include *Thunderball*, *GoldenEye*, *Tomorrow Never Dies*, and *Casino Royale*.

IN THE DRIVER'S SEAT

James Bond 007 is a fictional British agent created in 1952 by writer Ian Fleming. He is a tough guy who is always in control of any situation, but he is also a gentleman who enjoys the finer things in life. On the silver screen, he has been played by Sean Connery, George Lazenby, Roger Moore, Timothy Dalton, Pierce Brosnan, and Daniel Craig.

---

prototype: *first full-scale model of a new design*

? Ian Fleming chose "James Bond" because he wanted the simplest, plainest sounding name he could find. Why do you think he would want a dull name for such an exciting character? What do you think of when you hear the name James Bond?

Sean Connery as James Bond, with the famous Aston Martin in 1964

TRENDSETTER

There have been over 20 official James Bond movies to showcase 007's fantastic cars — leaving fans daydreaming about driving these hot rides. While Bond has driven other models throughout the years, Aston Martin is definitely the best fit for this sophisticated spy. This pairing gave the Aston Martin company more publicity than they ever could have achieved with an expensive advertising campaign.

? The Aston Martin featured in *Die Another Day* had a special switch that made it invisible. How do you think that could help a secret agent? How would you use that technology?

Quick Fact

Agent 007's famous introduction, "Bond, James Bond," became his catchphrase after it was first said by Sean Connery in *Dr. No*. Since then, it has entered the vocabulary of popular culture representing polished, understated machismo.

---

machismo: *exaggerated manliness*

BMT 216A

10   9   7   6

James Bond's car stolen from Boca airport

A newspaper article from the *Boca Raton News*, June 20, 1997
By Claire Booth

Under cover of darkness, someone entered a locked hangar in a secured area and made off with a priceless automobile. It was a feat worthy of James Bond.

But Bond hasn't driven this particular Aston Martin since 1965.

The specially outfitted silver roadster shared screen time with Sean Connery in *Goldfinger* in 1964 and in *Thunderball* the following year. The car has been spending most of its days at special exhibits and nights in a Boca Raton Airport hangar.

That is, until Wednesday. Someone sliced through the molding on the hangar door, cut the metal latch and snipped the alarm wires sometime between 4 PM Wednesday and 7 AM Thursday. There was no key in the car, according to police reports, so the burglar either hot-wired the 1963 Aston Martin DB5 or simply pushed it out of the hangar and into the night.

"It's really kind of wild that someone had the nerve to steal it," said Anthony Pugliese, who has owned the car since 1986. "What are they going to do with it?"

If the right-hand steering and European-style license plates don't catch the eye of fellow motorists, the roadster's optional accessories certainly will. Not many cars come equipped with a bulletproof rear window, passenger-side ejection seat, and machine guns.

"It's a one-of-a-kind," Pugliese said, disbelief over the theft still clear in his voice. "It's the most famous car in the world, an icon of the '60s." …

The Expert Says…

" They are an extension of his [Bond's] powerful and suave personality and often the means by which he achieves his freedom. "

— Robert Thompson, professor of Media and Culture, Syracuse University

suave: *sophisticated; charming*

Take Note

Bond's Aston Martin takes the #2 spot on our list. The success of the James Bond movie franchise not only benefits Hollywood, but the pairing with Aston Martin makes it one of the most popular cars on the market. This has made other companies very eager to feature their products in movies.
• What do you think should be considered when trying to match the right product to the right movie character?

5   4   3   **2**   1

The designers wanted this Batmobile to be an extraordinary machine that no one had ever seen before. It is from 1989's *Batman* — the most financially successful film of the Batman franchise (so far).

DEBUT: The Batmobile made its first appearance in 1941 in the pages of DC Comics' Batman #5.

MAKE/MODEL: It began as a red sedan, but has transformed into a futuristic vehicle with just about every high-tech gadget you could imagine.

Whether or not you have read the comic book, watched the TV show, or seen the latest *Batman* movie, you have undoubtedly heard of the Caped Crusader's famous ride.

Who wouldn't love a car equipped with an ejector seat to escape rush-hour traffic? Throw in some jet thrusters, machine guns, and a video-conferencing screen and you've got a pretty sweet ride. When it comes to fighting crime, gadgets are a definite must-have. This is especially true with Batman, who doesn't have any superhuman powers. Luckily, the Caped Crusader's contraptions are so cool that even the Joker had to ask, "Where does he get those wonderful toys?"

The "toy" that comes in at #1 on our list is the Batmobile. Whether it's speeding to the scene of a crime or flying through a waterfall, this ride is the Dark Knight's best-known weapon. Since its comic-book debut more than 60 years ago, the Batmobile has had many different looks and features. All versions have a few things in common, though. They look incredible, are technologically advanced, and are packed with jaw-dropping gadgets.

The Hollywood versions of the Batmobile are especially amazing because they have to function fully to be believable onscreen. Whether you're talking about the car from the campy 1960s TV series, or the bizarre tank-like Tumbler in 2005's *Batman Begins*, the Batmobile is an important part of the Batman legend.

campy: *deliberately cheesy or silly*

THE BATMOBILE

A STAR IS BORN

Many people still think of the car from the 1960s TV series as *the* Batmobile. This futuristic street machine was created by George Barris, who also worked on James Dean's Spyder. Barris modified a rejected concept car called the Lincoln Futura by adding bat-like fins, a cool paint job, and some amazing gadgets. The next most popular Batmobile is from the 1989 film, *Batman*. This menacing machine was designed to look like a combination of a stealth aircraft and a medieval knight in armor.

IN THE DRIVER'S SEAT

Batman is considered one of the greatest and most popular superheroes of all time. Because he is a regular human being, he gets his super abilities through ingenuity and technology. His alter ego is Bruce Wayne, a billionaire philanthropist who decides to fight crime after his parents are murdered. As Batman's look has changed through the years — from the bumbling man-in-tights to the handsome Christian Bale — he is considered a reflection of how our society also changes.

concept car: *experimental car usually shown at auto shows to find out customer reactions to new designs*

philanthropist: *someone who devotes his or her time to helping others*

TRENDSETTER

Over the years, the Batmobile has transformed along with its owner. The 1960s show may have been silly, but audiences had never seen a full-sized Batmobile tricked out with so many functioning gadgets. The 1989 version introduced the age of the big-budget comic-book based film. After watching this box-office blockbuster, suddenly every kid wanted a toy Batmobile. The movie created an unbelievable half-billion dollars in merchandise sales. It also paved the way for more sequels, bigger budgets and, of course, new Batmobile designs to keep people excited about the franchise.

? Some fans believe that superhero cars and suits keep changing so that new toys can be made. How do you feel about the role of merchandise sales? Are they a good or bad thing? Explain.

VROOOOOOM!

Adam West sits behind the wheel of the Batmobile from the 1960s TV series. This car sold at auction for $233,000 in March 2007.

The Expert Says...

[P]eople love our older Batmobile because it's not too sleek. It's fun. … And we did have the world's first car phone.

— Adam West, actor, played Batman in the 1960s television series

10   9   8   7   6

REINVENTING THE BATMOBILE

A labeled diagram from *Popular Mechanics*, July 2005
By Ron Magid

Director Chris Nolan demanded a unique Batmobile for *Batman Begins*. "Something as low as a Lamborghini, as aggressive and armored as a Hummer," says production designer Nathan Crowley. …

Crowley hit the toy stores, grabbed several models — Humvees, Countachs, P-38s — then "smashed those kits together." … The result: the world's first sports tank.

FACETED DESIGN
The Batmobile's faceted "armor plating" is a visual jambalaya of angular design cues.

jambalaya: *way of saying mixture (based on a Creole stew)*

BEHIND THE SCENES:
Transforming the sleek Bat-vehicles of yore into a sports tank

yore: *past*

INDEPENDENTLY MOUNTED FRONT WHEELS
"The director wanted the front wheels to look like two clenched fists."

? This car has also been compared to a military vehicle that is used in Iraq. Do you think this was done as a reflection of the state of the world in 2005? Explain.

REAR FLAPS
Faux jet engine and aerodynamic rear flaps.

faux: *imitation; artificial*

Take Note

The Batmobile earns the #1 spot on our list. This car has the looks, the features, and a superhero driver. It has become a part of our popular imagination.
• Why do you think the Batmobile has changed so much in design and appearance over the years? How do you think its changing design helped to earn it the #1 spot on our list?

MASSIVE REAR WHEELS
Two pairs of 44-inch superswamper tires — one pair on either side of the car's fake jet engine — provide go-anywhere traction.

5   4   3   2   1

We Thought ...

Here are the criteria we used in ranking the 10 hottest Hollywood cars.

The car:
- Has cool gadgets
- Performs daring stunts
- Makes a unique statement
- Has had a huge impact on popular culture
- Is paired with an extraordinary driver
- Influences the design of other cars
- Has been used in mind-blowing stunt scenes
- Has contributed to the success of a film or television show
- Has achieved a legendary status

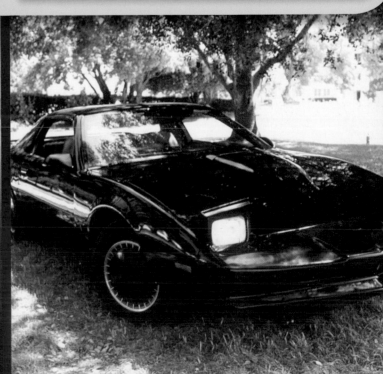

What Do You Think?

1. Do you agree with our ranking? If you don't, try ranking these cars yourself. Justify your ranking with data from your own research and reasoning. You may refer to our criteria, or you may want to draw up your own list of criteria.

2. Here are three other cars that we considered, but in the end did not include in our top 10 list: Delorean from *Back to the Future*, Plymouth from *Christine*, and the General Lee from the *Dukes of Hazzard*.
   • Find out more about these cars. Do you think they should have made our list? Give reasons for your response.
   • Are there other cars that you think should have made our list? Explain your choices.

Index